MEAN COLORING BOOKS

A REAL ADULT COLORING BOOK

I ~~HATE~~ LOVE MY JOB

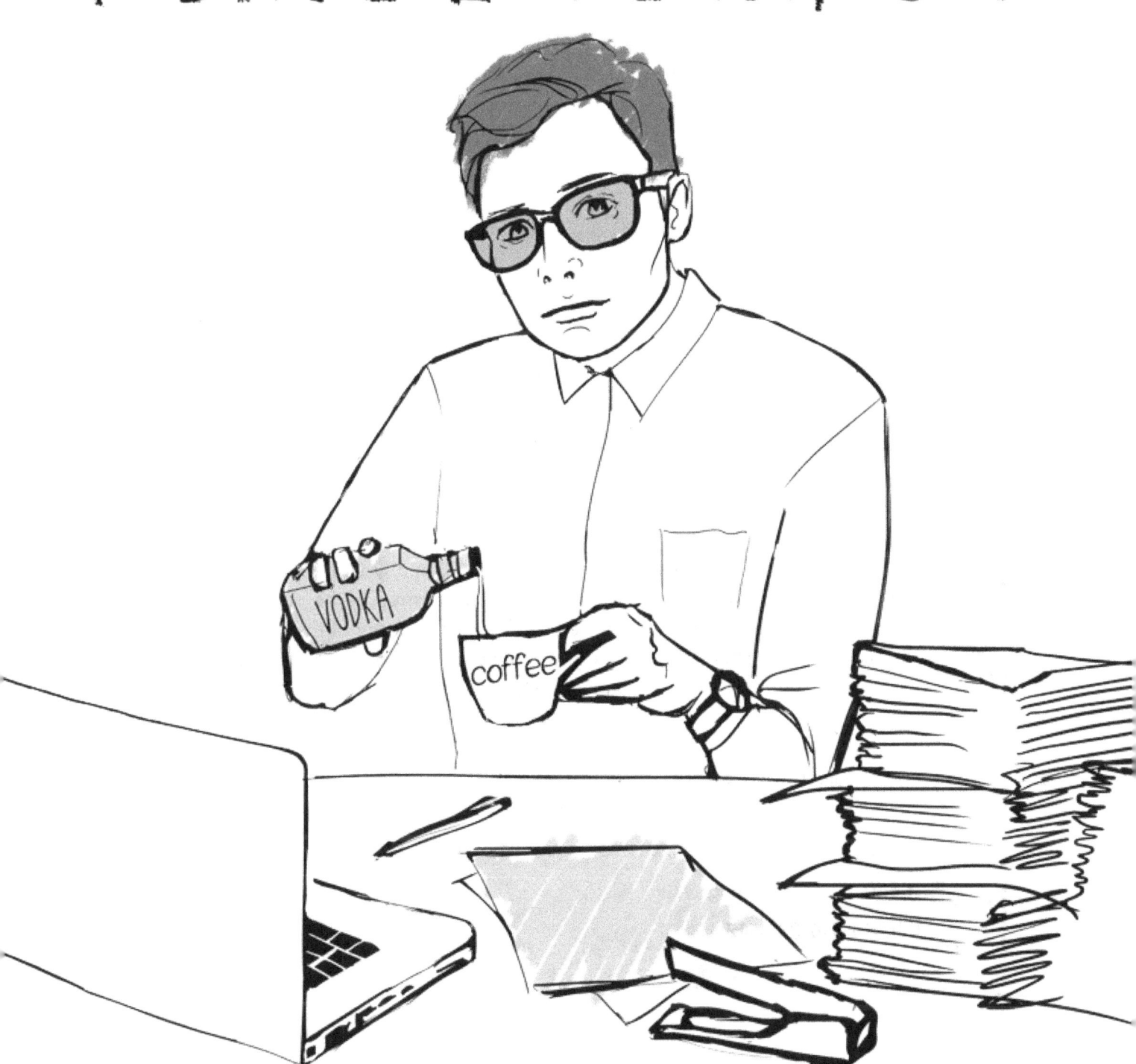

Author: Nadia Sotnikova
Interior Design: Kristina Tosic

Published by: Go Fox Media, LP / Glasgow, Scotland

First Edition, First Printing

ISBN: 978-1-61343-114-6

How to ^NOT To Deal with Stress at Work

A REAL ADULT COLORING BOOK

Go Fox Media / Scotland

After years of dealing with daily stress at work, I decided it was time to take this issue out of the closet and start talking about it openly. We're stressed. It sucks. Let's do something about it!

This real adult coloring book is a great way to open a conversation about stress at work, get creative and have fun.

Relax and enjoy!

Nadia Sotnikova.
nadia@gofoxmedia.com

ARE YOU USED TO SAYING "YES" TO EVERY PROJECT THAT COMES YOUR WAY? EVEN THOUGH IT'S IMPORTANT TO HELP YOUR COLLEAGUES, YOU CAN HANDLE ONLY SO MUCH WORK AT A TIME.

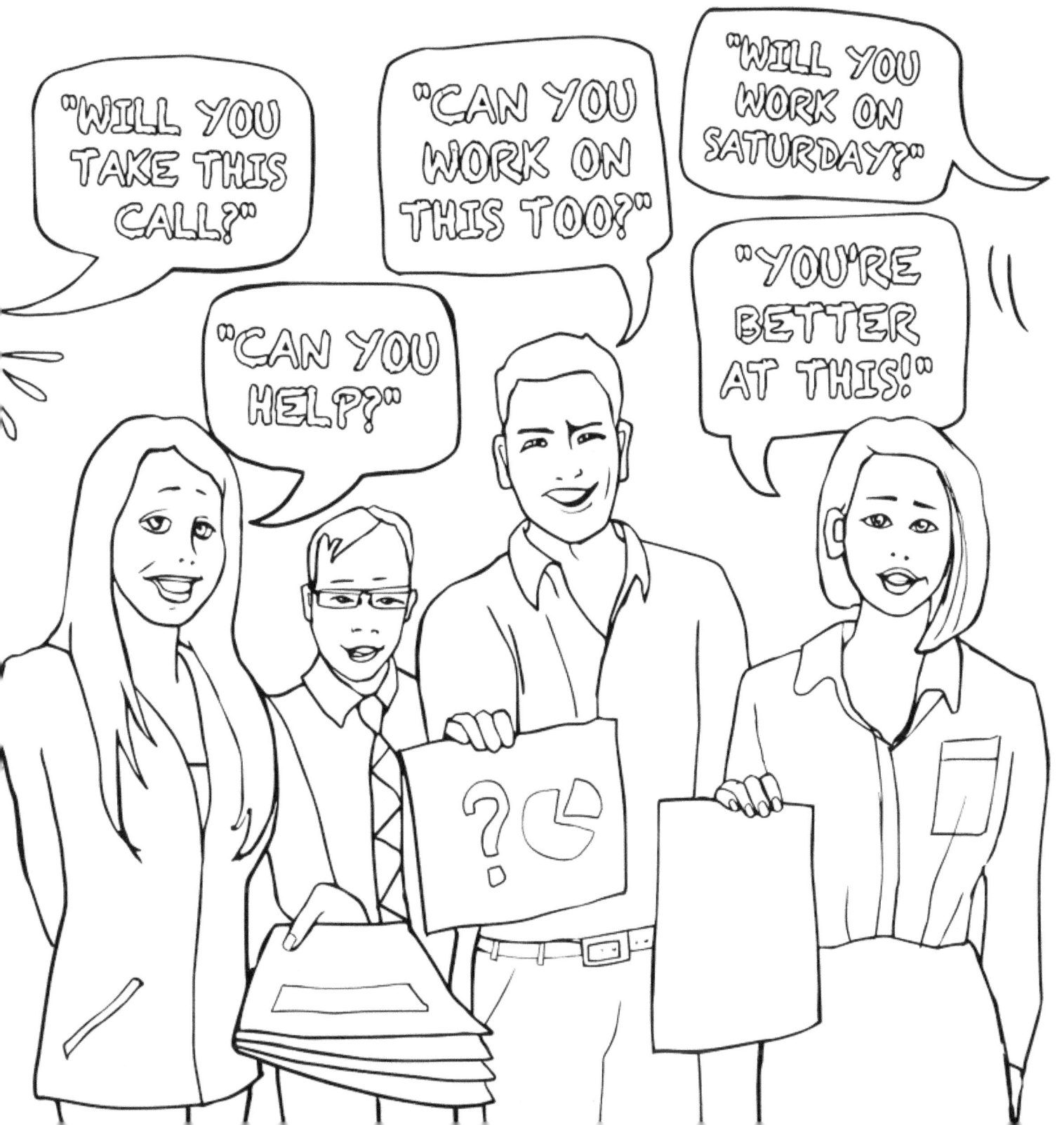

YOU MAY CONSIDER YOURSELF THE QUEEN OR THE KING OF MULTITASKING, BUT LET'S BE HONEST, YOU'RE NOT. MULTITASKING CAN ACTUALLY CONTRIBUTE TO YOUR STRESS AND INABILITY TO RELAX.

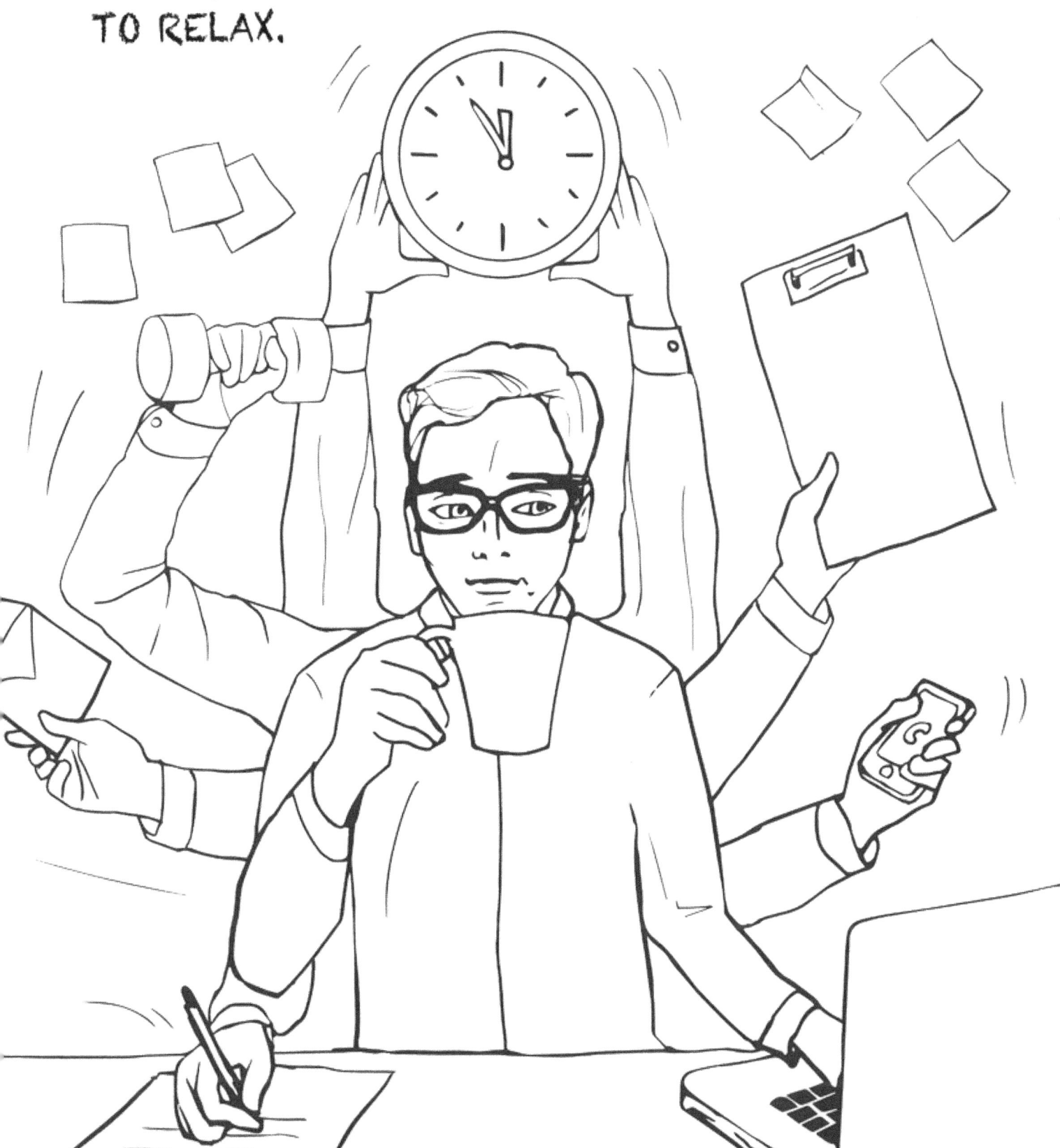

YOU WAKE UP FEELING SICK. DO YOU COME TO WORK, OR DO YOU STAY HOME? IT'S COMMON FOR WORKERS TO FEEL GUILTY WHEN TAKING A SICK DAY. HOWEVER, CHOOSING TO WORK DESPITE FEELING ILL CAN WORSEN YOUR CONDITION, INCREASE STRESS, AND GET YOUR COWORKERS SICK TOO.

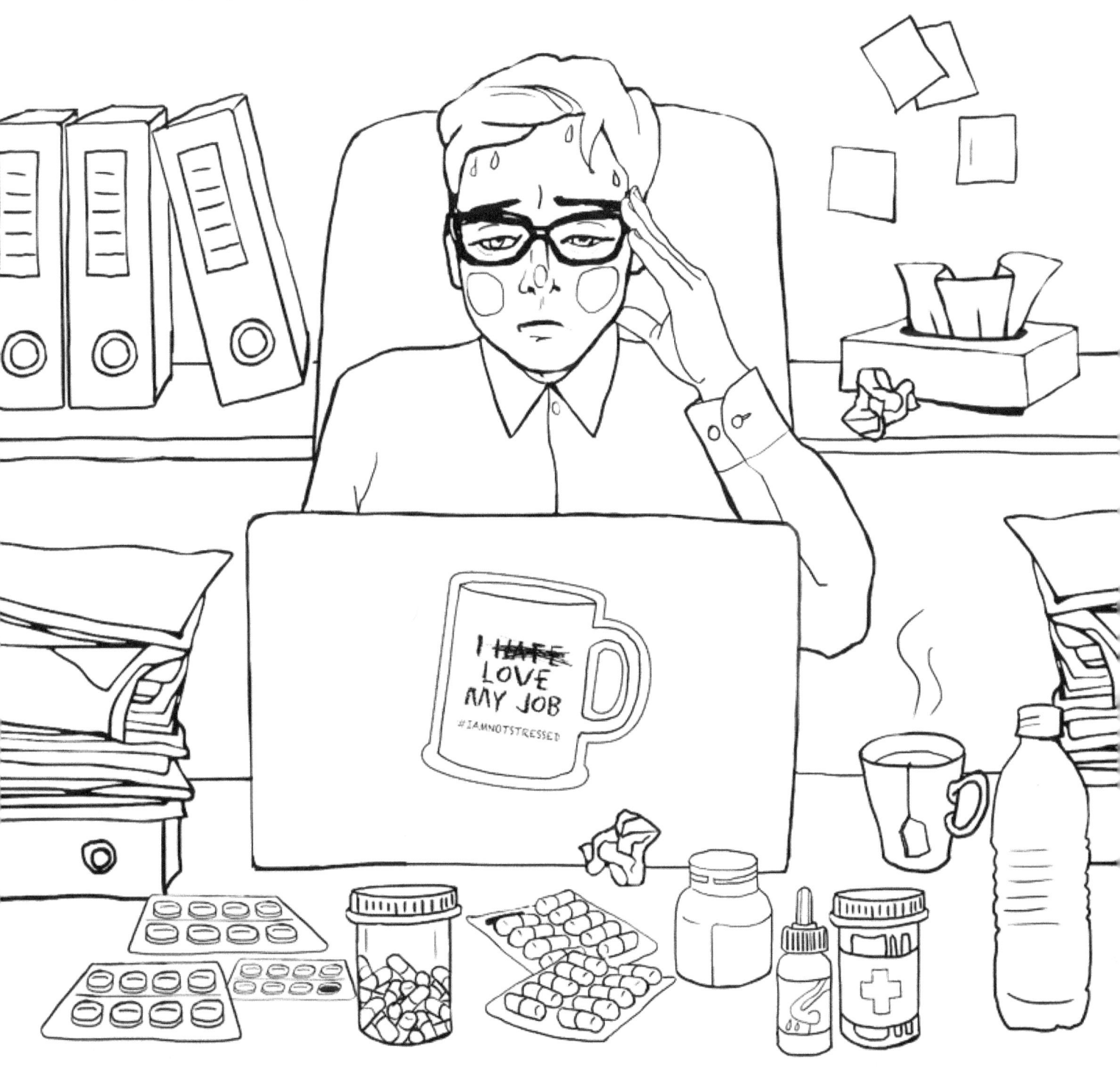

IT TAKES TIME GETTING USED TO WORKING WITH A NEW TEAM. MORE OFTEN THAN NOT, STRESS ON THE TEAM COMES FROM POOR COMMUNICATION. HOW WOULD YOU RESOLVE A CONFLICT BETWEEN YOU AND YOUR TEAM MEMBERS? THE FIRST STEPS TO RESOLVING ANY CONFLICT IS ACKNOWLEDGING THE FACT THAT CONFLICT EXISTS AND BEING TRANSPARENT WHEN TALKING ABOUT IT.

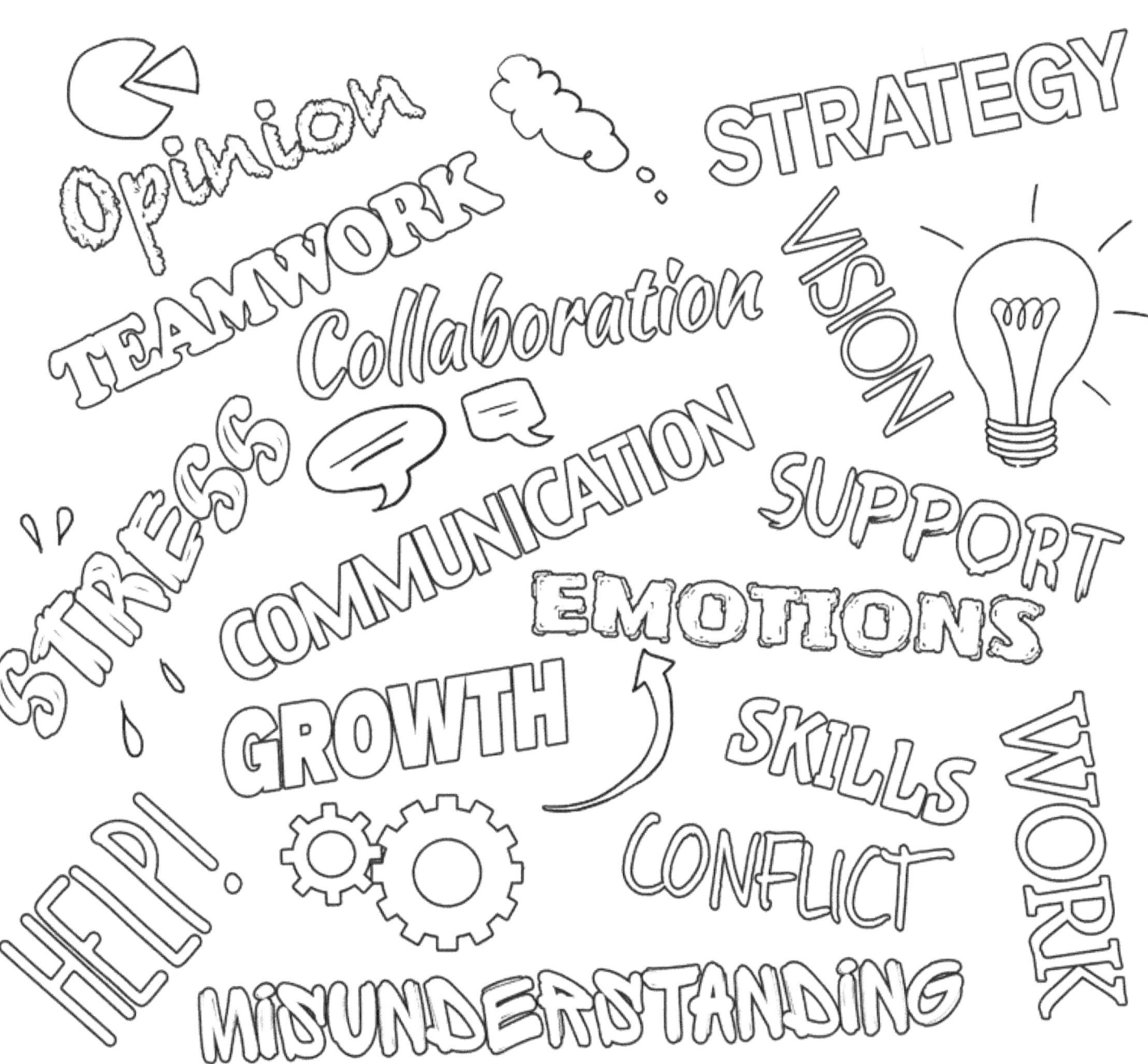

ISSUES LIKE ANXIETY OR DEPRESSION CAN MAKE WORK DIFFICULT, ESPECIALLY WHEN YOU'RE WORKING UNDER A LOT OF PRESSURE. IT'S IMPORTANT TO SEEK HELP AND DIFFERENTIATE BETWEEN WORK STRESS AND MORE SERIOUS ISSUES.

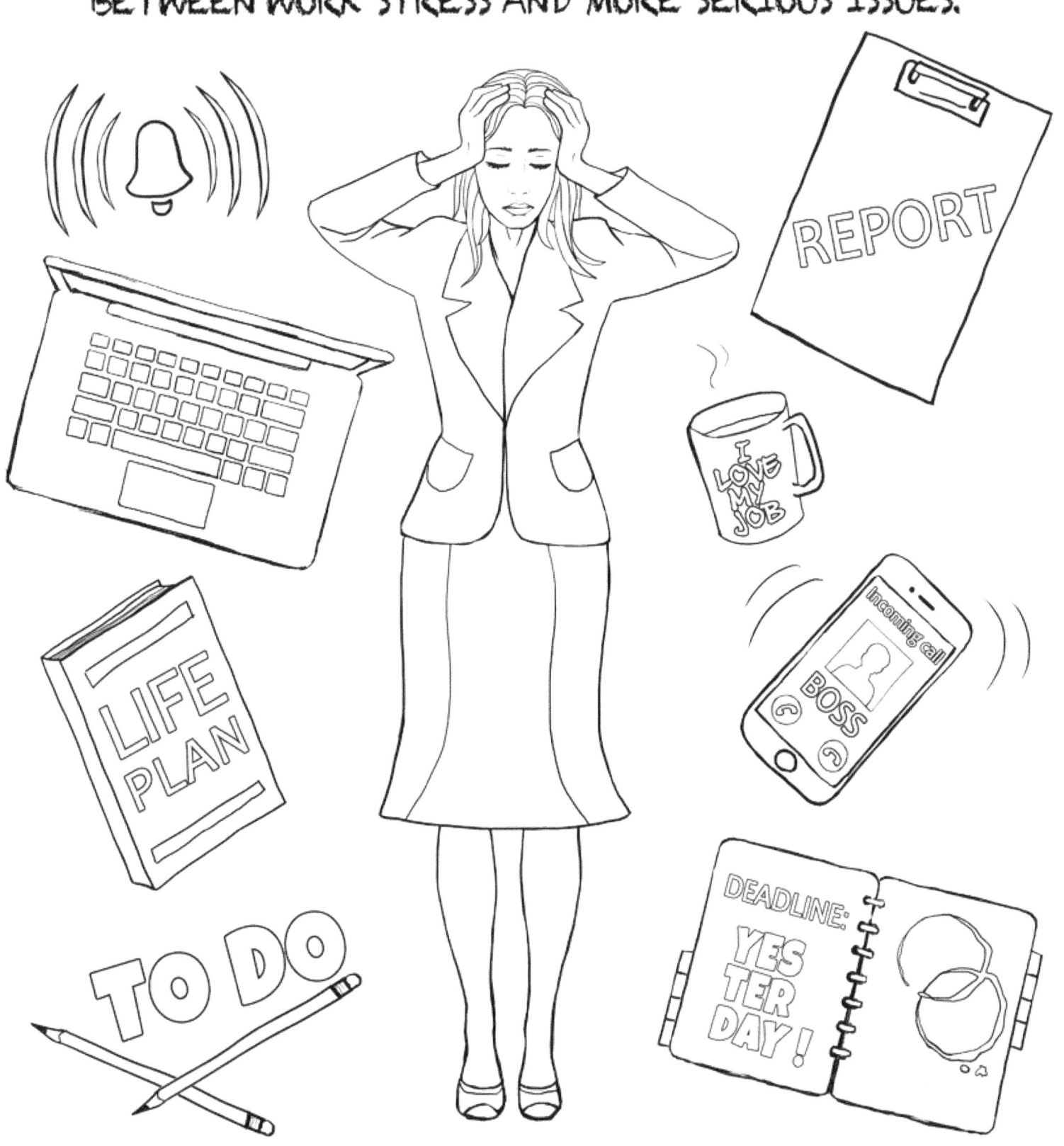

INNOVATION AND FAILURE GO HAND-IN-HAND, BUT NOT ALL TEAMS ARE SUPPORTIVE WHEN IT COMES TO MAKING MISTAKES. THE FEAR OF FAILURE CAN LEAVE YOU EXTREMELY STRESSED. HAVE YOU EVER BEEN A PART OF BLAME CULTURE?

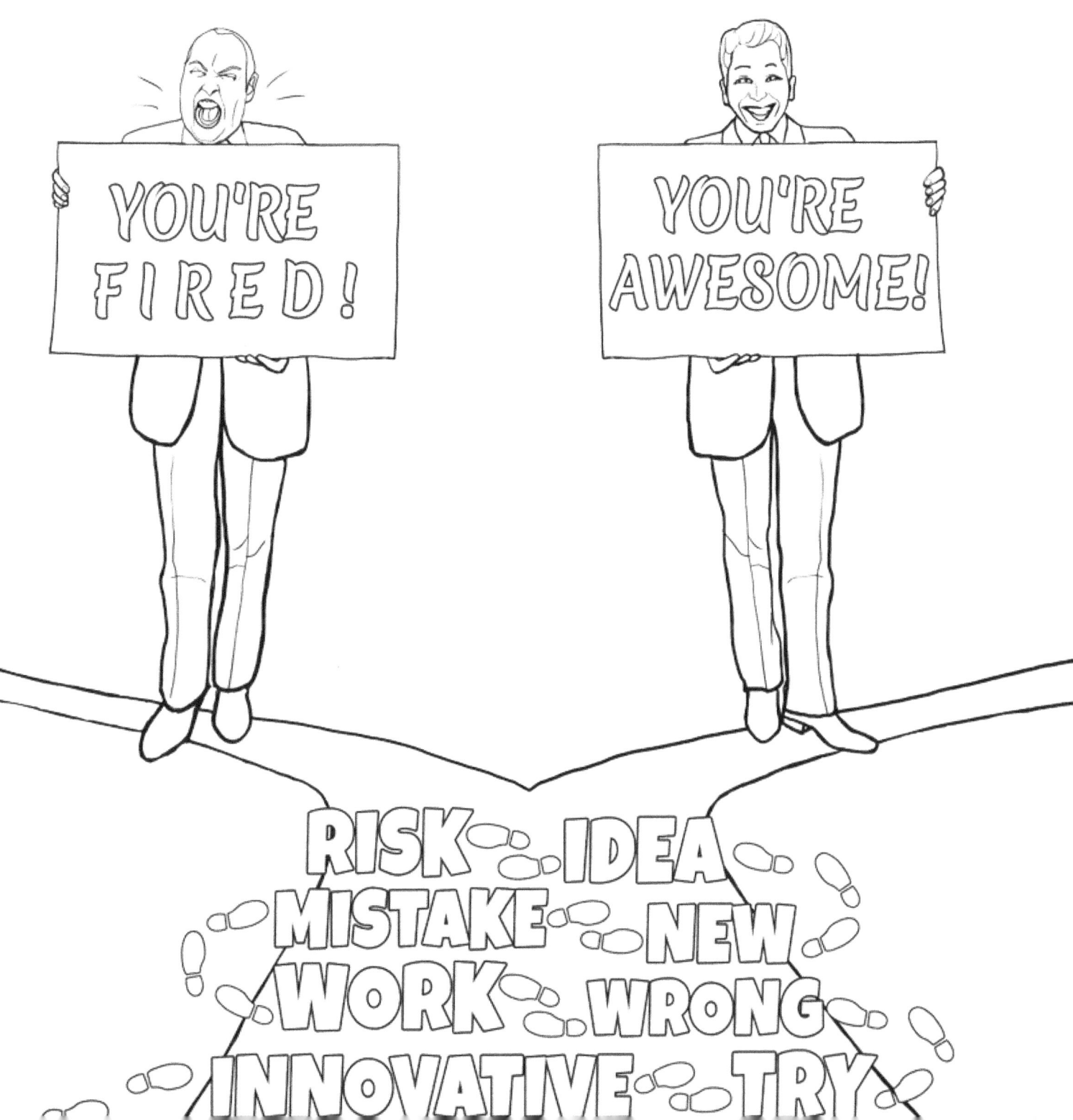

HAVE YOU EVER WORKED WITH A BULLY? BULLYING AT WORK OFTEN GOES UNNOTICED, ESPECIALLY IF IT'S COMING FROM YOUR MANAGERS OR CLIENTS. YOU CAN IGNORE IT AND SUFFER IN SILENCE, OR YOU CAN SPEAK UP. WHAT WOULD YOU DO?

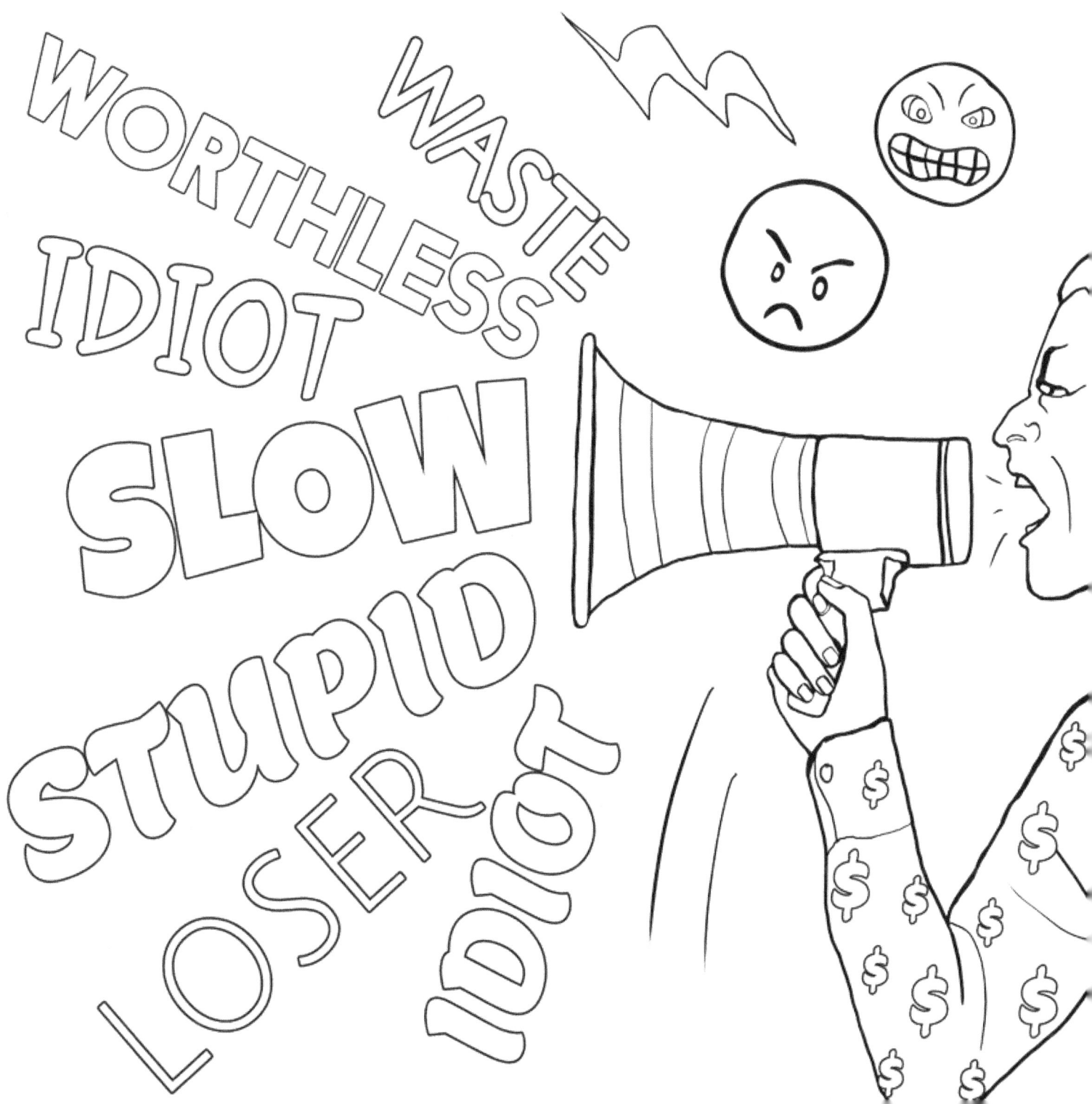

POOR MANAGEMENT CAN LEAD TO A LOT OF STRESS. CONFLICTING DIRECTIONS AND LACK OF FEEDBACK CAN MAKE YOU FEEL OUT OF CONTROL AND LEAVE YOU UNABLE TO DO YOUR BEST WORK. HOW WOULD YOU DEAL WITH A SITUATION LIKE THIS?

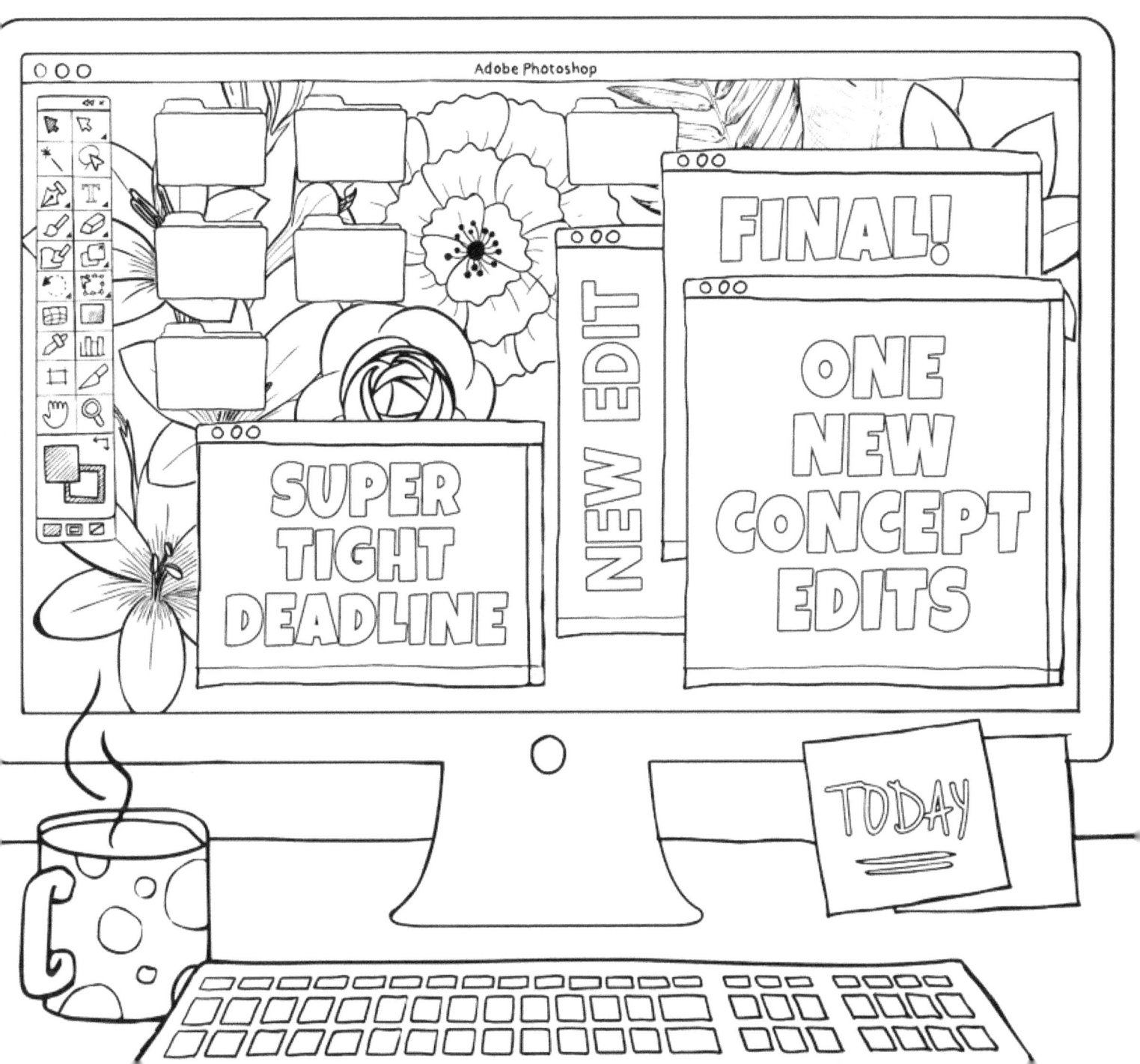

IT'S AS IMPORTANT TO PREVENT WORK STRESS FROM AFFECTING YOUR HOME LIFE AS IT IS KEEPING YOUR HOME STRESS FROM AFFECTING YOUR WORK LIFE. WHAT IS YOUR REAL SOURCE OF STRESS?

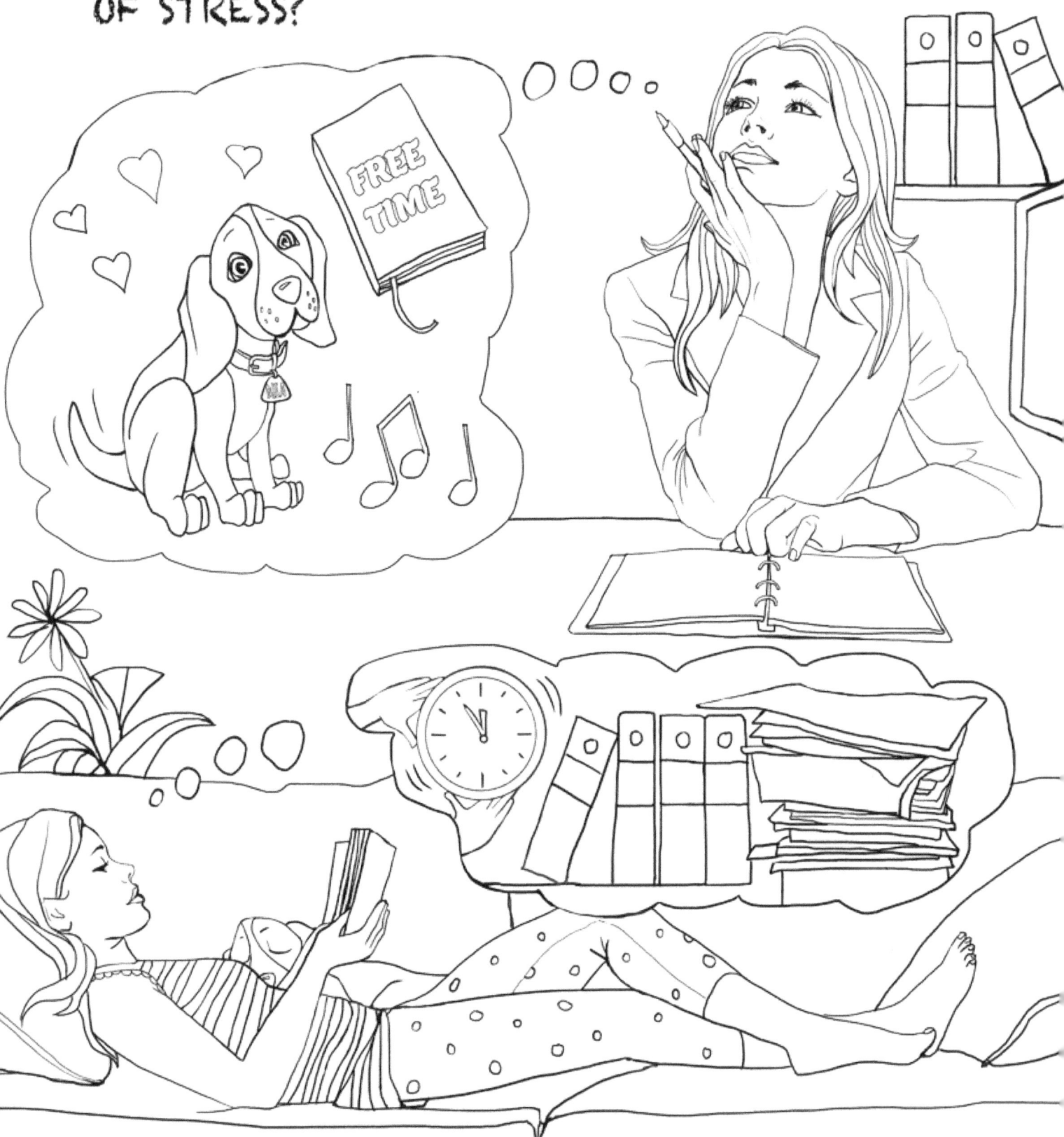

STRESS CAN BE EMOTIONALLY AND PHYSICALLY DRAINING. DO YOU FIND YOURSELF REACHING FOR COFFEE MORE OFTEN WHEN YOU'RE UNDER A LOT OF PRESSURE? CONSUMING TOO MUCH CAFFEINE CAN GET YOU THROUGH A LONG DAY AT WORK, BUT IT MAY ALSO KEEP YOU AWAKE AT NIGHT AND MAKE YOU EVEN MORE TIRED.

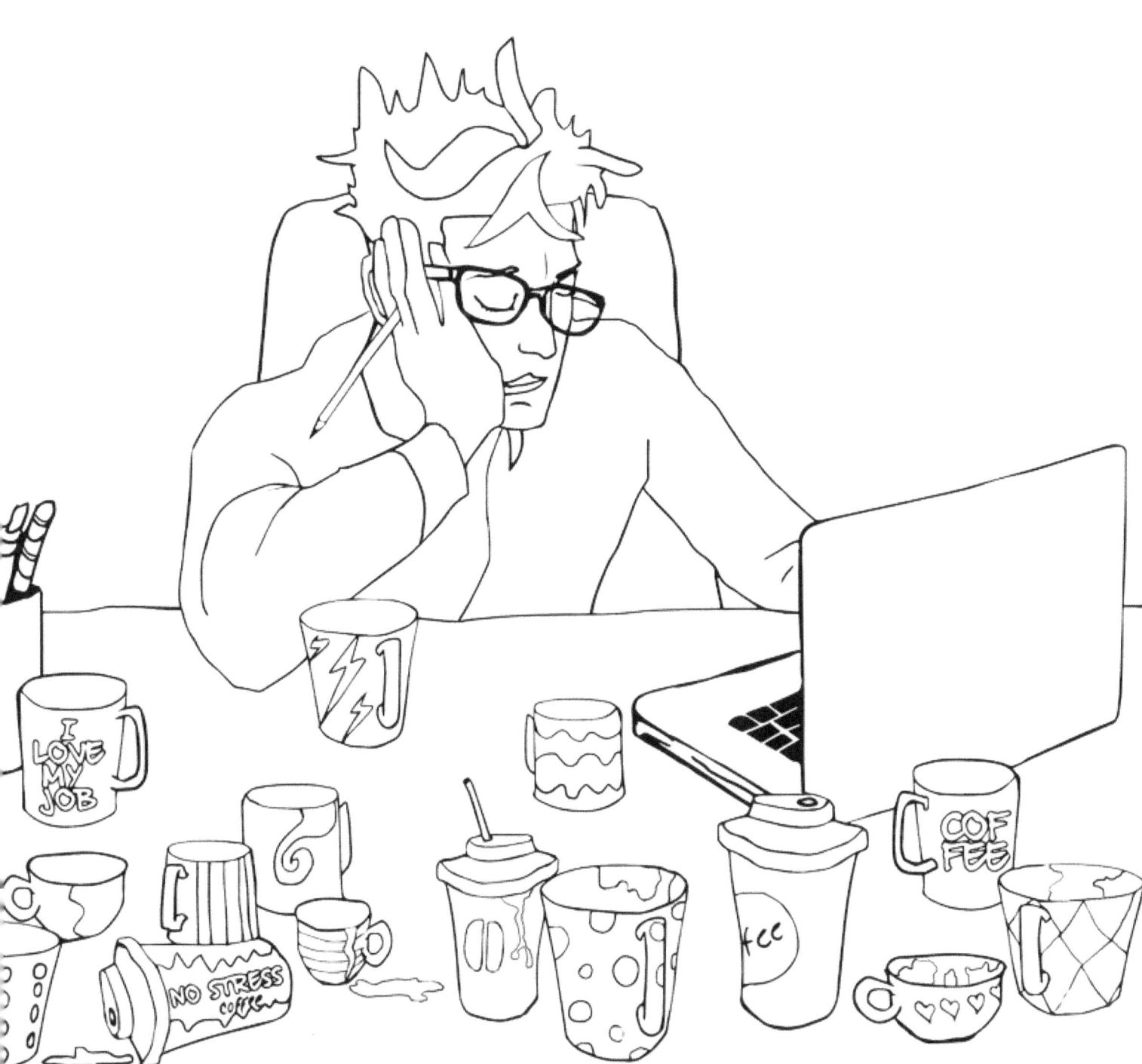

IT'S HARD TO STAY MOTIVATED AND GET YOURSELF TO EXERCISE WHEN YOU'RE STRESSED. HOWEVER, EXERCISING CAN HELP YOU CLEAR YOUR MIND AND STAY ENERGIZED THROUGHOUT THE DAY. HOW DOES YOUR BODY RESPOND WHEN YOU'RE STRESSED? DO YOU FEEL THE NEED TO MOVE, OR DO YOU FEEL "PARALYZED"?

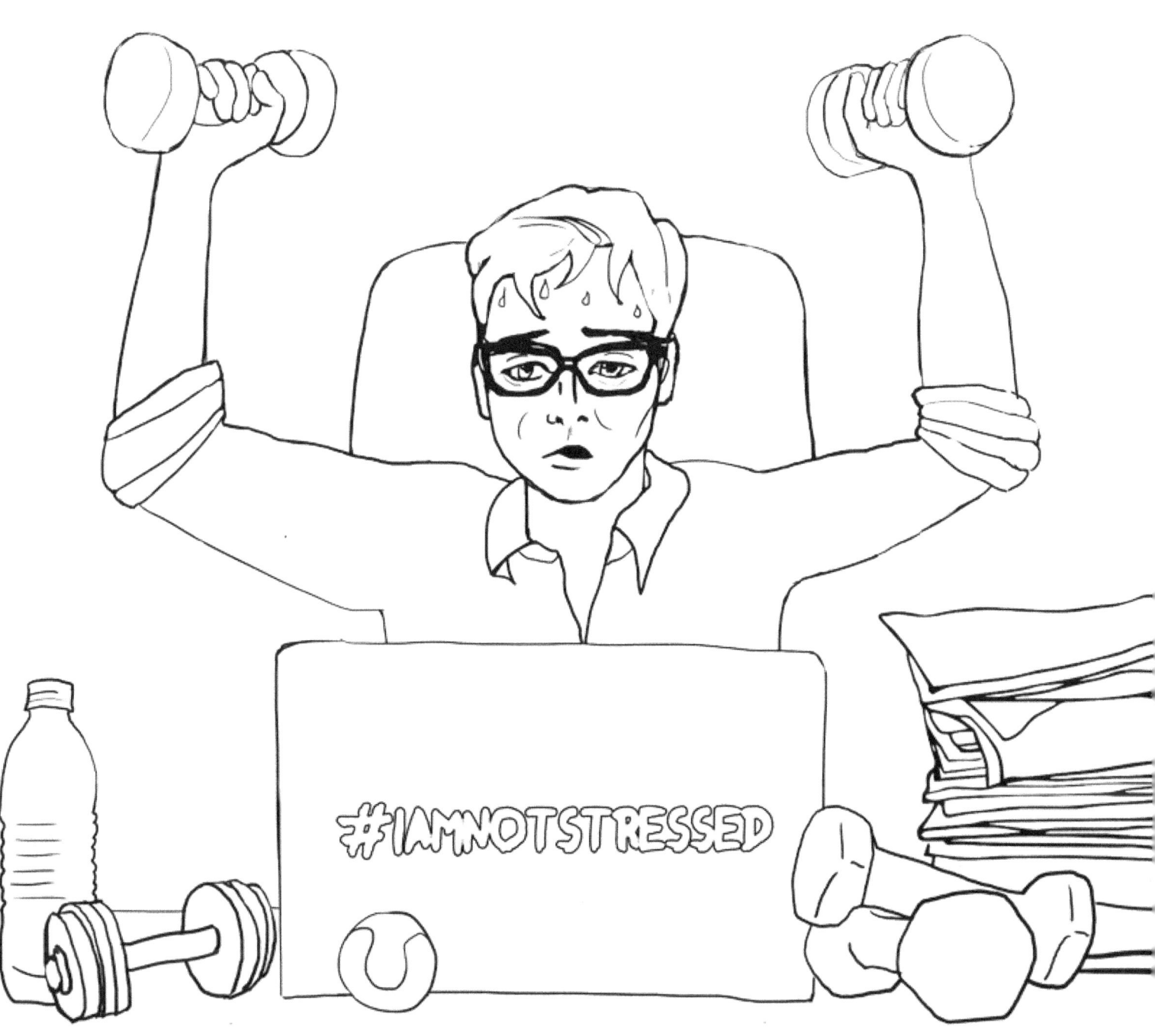

HOW DO YOU DEAL WITH EXTREMELY SHORT DEADLINES? DO YOU FREEZE, OR DO YOU BECOME MORE FOCUSED AND PRODUCTIVE? UNREALISTIC DEADLINES CAN PUT YOU UNDER A LOT OF PRESSURE. IF YOU STRUGGLE WITH FINISHING WORK ON TIME, THE ISSUE COULD BE POOR PLANNING OR INEFFICIENT PROJECT MANAGEMENT.

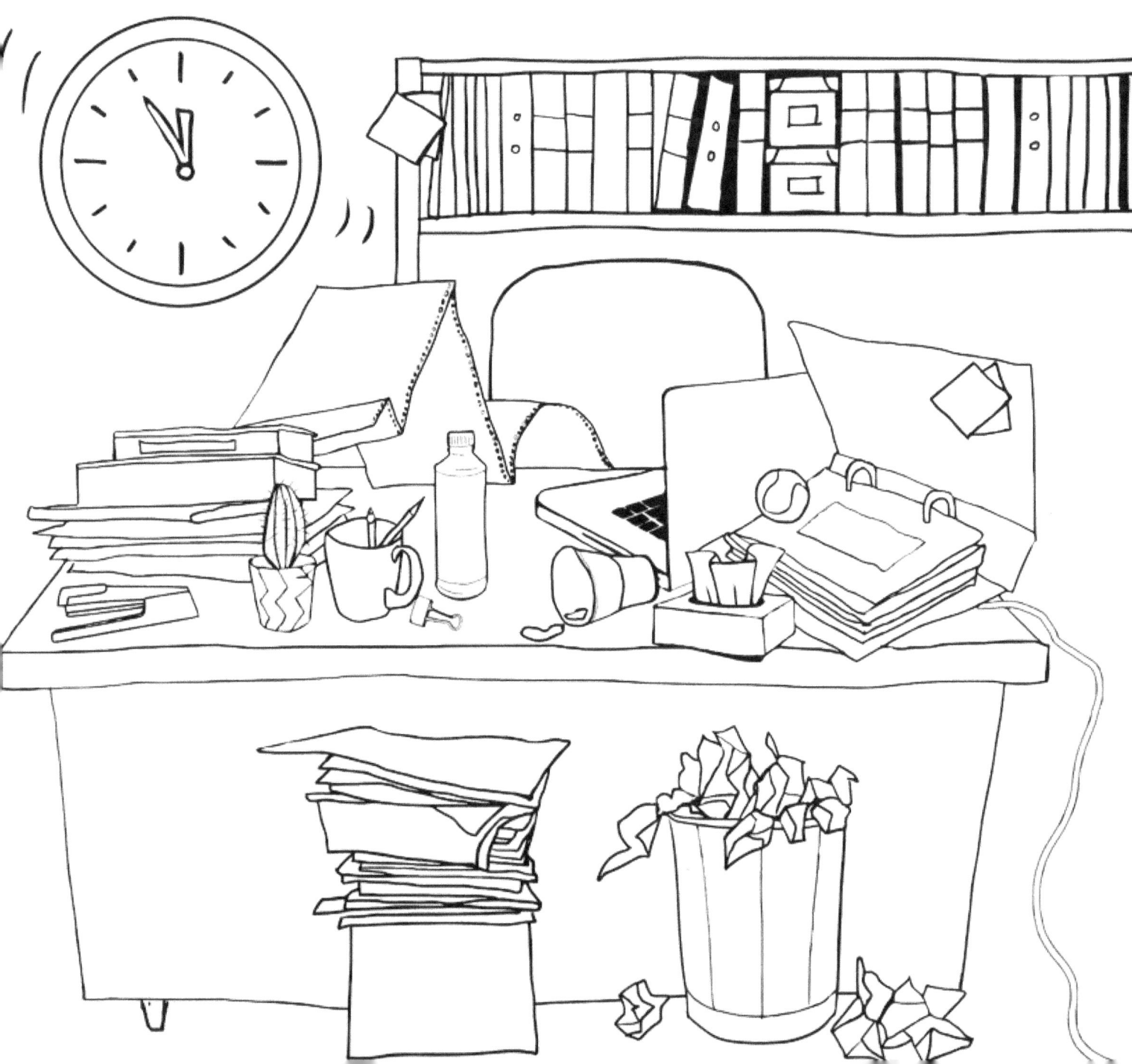

TOO MUCH COMFORT FOOD CAN CAUSE MORE DISCOMFORT. TRY HERBAL TEAS AND HEALTHY SNACKS TO KEEP YOUR ENERGY LEVELS HIGH AND STRESS LEVELS LOW!

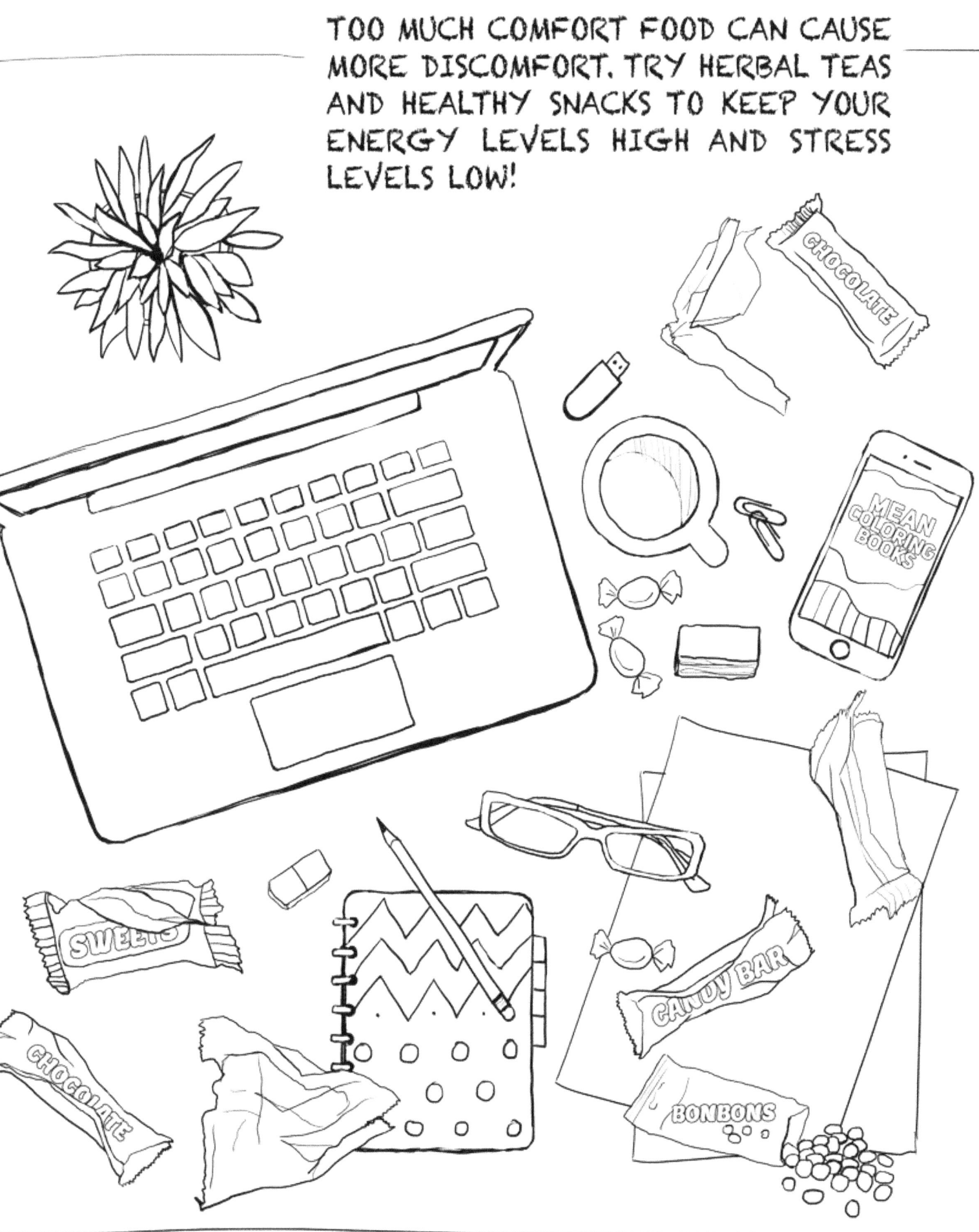

PROCRASTINATING ON SOCIAL MEDIA WON'T HELP YOUR STRESS LEVELS, ESPECIALLY IF YOUR BOSS CATCHES YOU BROWSING FACEBOOK AT 10AM ON MONDAY. TAKING A 10 MINUTE BREAK AWAY FROM YOUR COMPUTER WOULD BE A MUCH BETTER SOLUTION, EVEN IF IT'S JUST A QUICK RUN TO THE WATER COOLER.

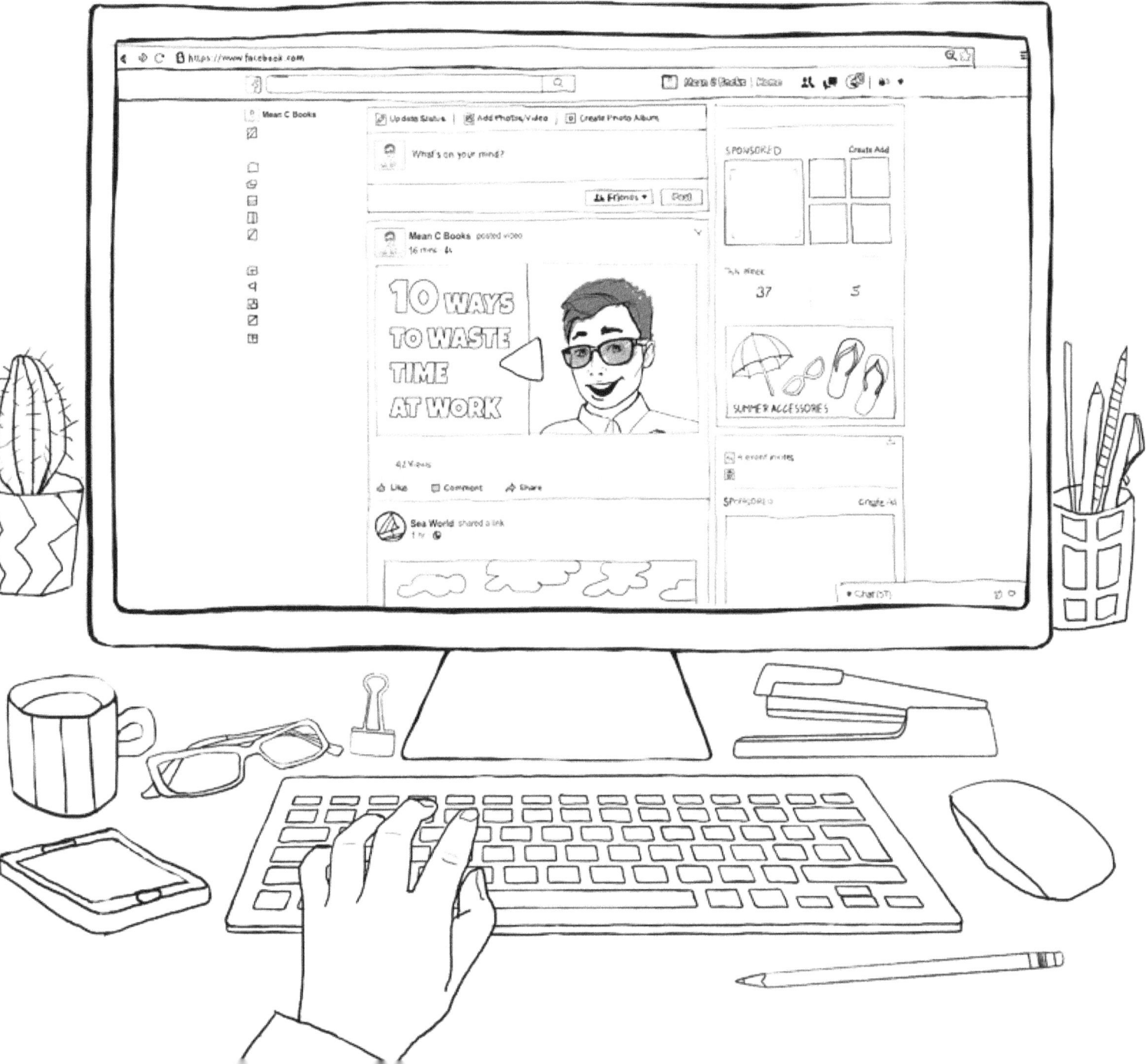

WHEN STRESSED, YOU MAY FEEL TEMPTED TO ISOLATE YOURSELF FROM THE PEOPLE YOU WORK WITH. WHILE IT'S SOMETIMES NECESSARY TO BE ALONE FOR A WHILE, HIDING YOUR FEELINGS FROM OTHERS IS NOT A GOOD IDEA. IF YOU'RE FEELING COMPLETELY OVERWHELMED, LET YOUR MANAGER KNOW! DON'T SUFFER IN SILENCE.

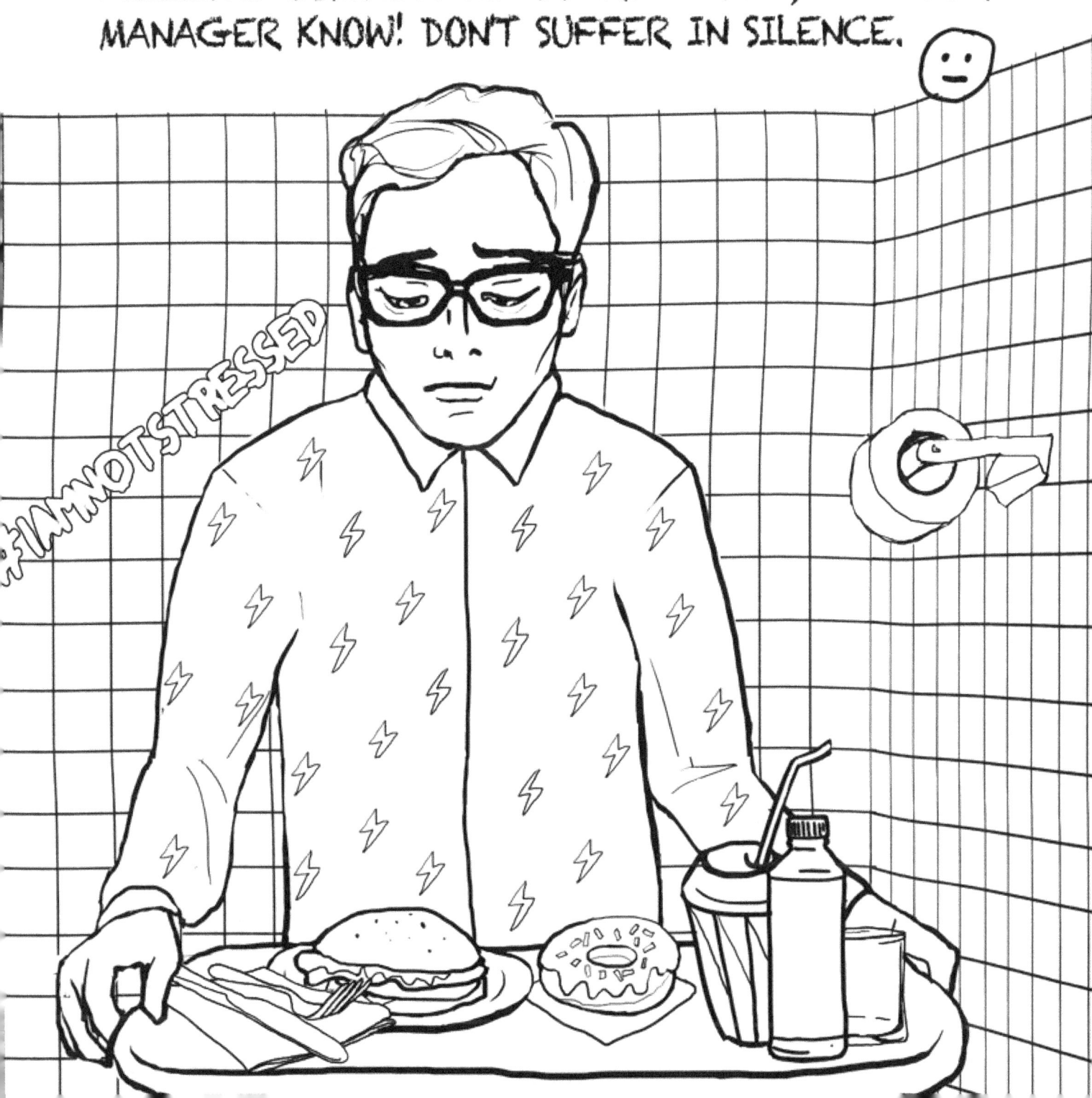

KEEPING YOUR EMOTIONS UNDER CONTROL IS NORMAL. REPRESSING THEM COMPLETELY IS NOT. ONE DAY YOU WILL BLOW UP AND THINGS WILL GET UGLY. HANDLE ISSUES WHEN THEY ARISE, AND YOU WILL AVOID A LOT OF CONFLICT LATER.

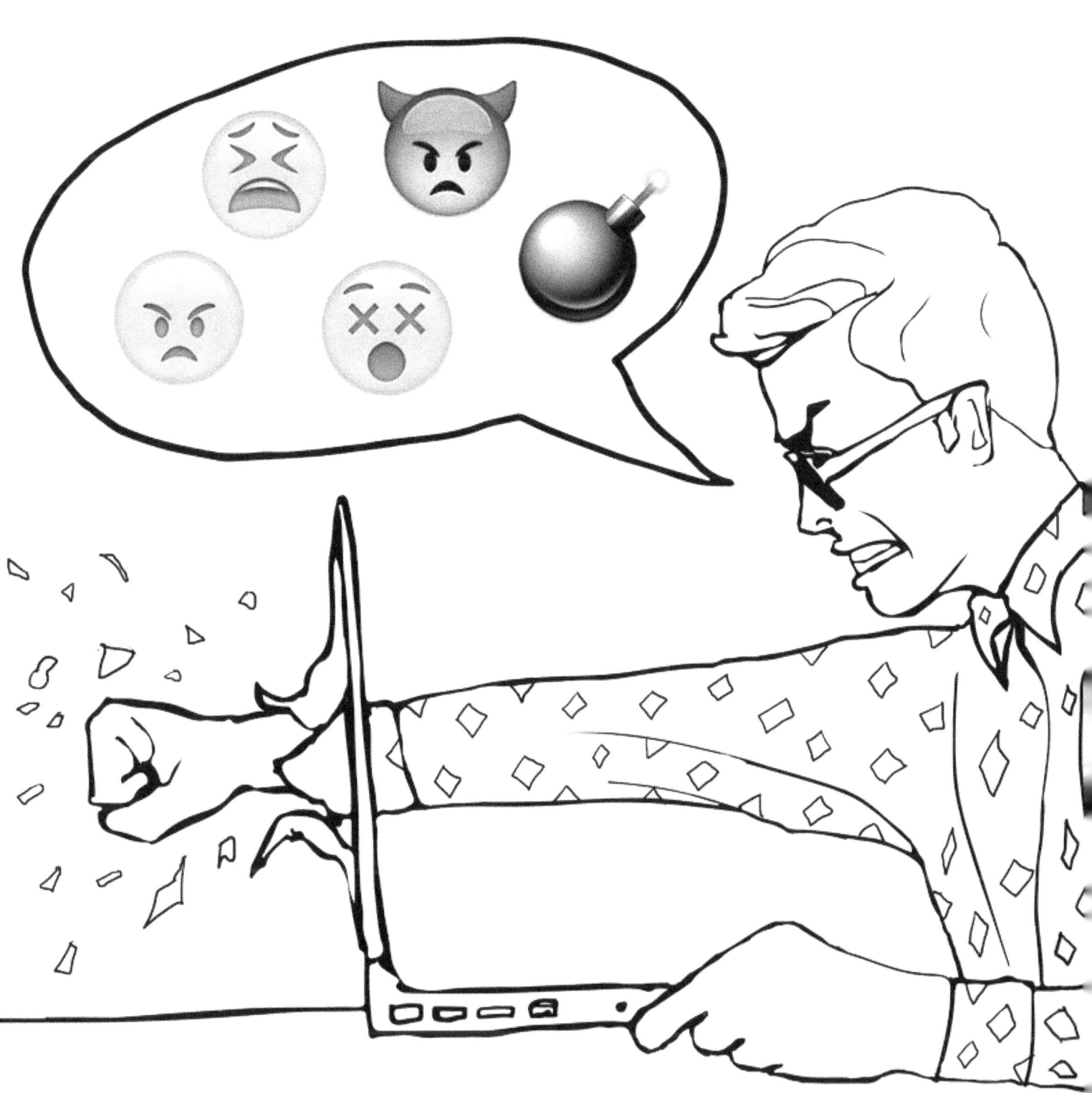

FROM TIME TO TIME, WE ALL FIND OURSELVES IN A CRISIS SITUATION WHEN THINGS JUST AREN'T GOING AS PLANNED. HOW DO YOU DEAL WITH SUCH SHORT-TERM STRESS TO STAY GROUNDED AND MAKE GOOD DECISIONS?

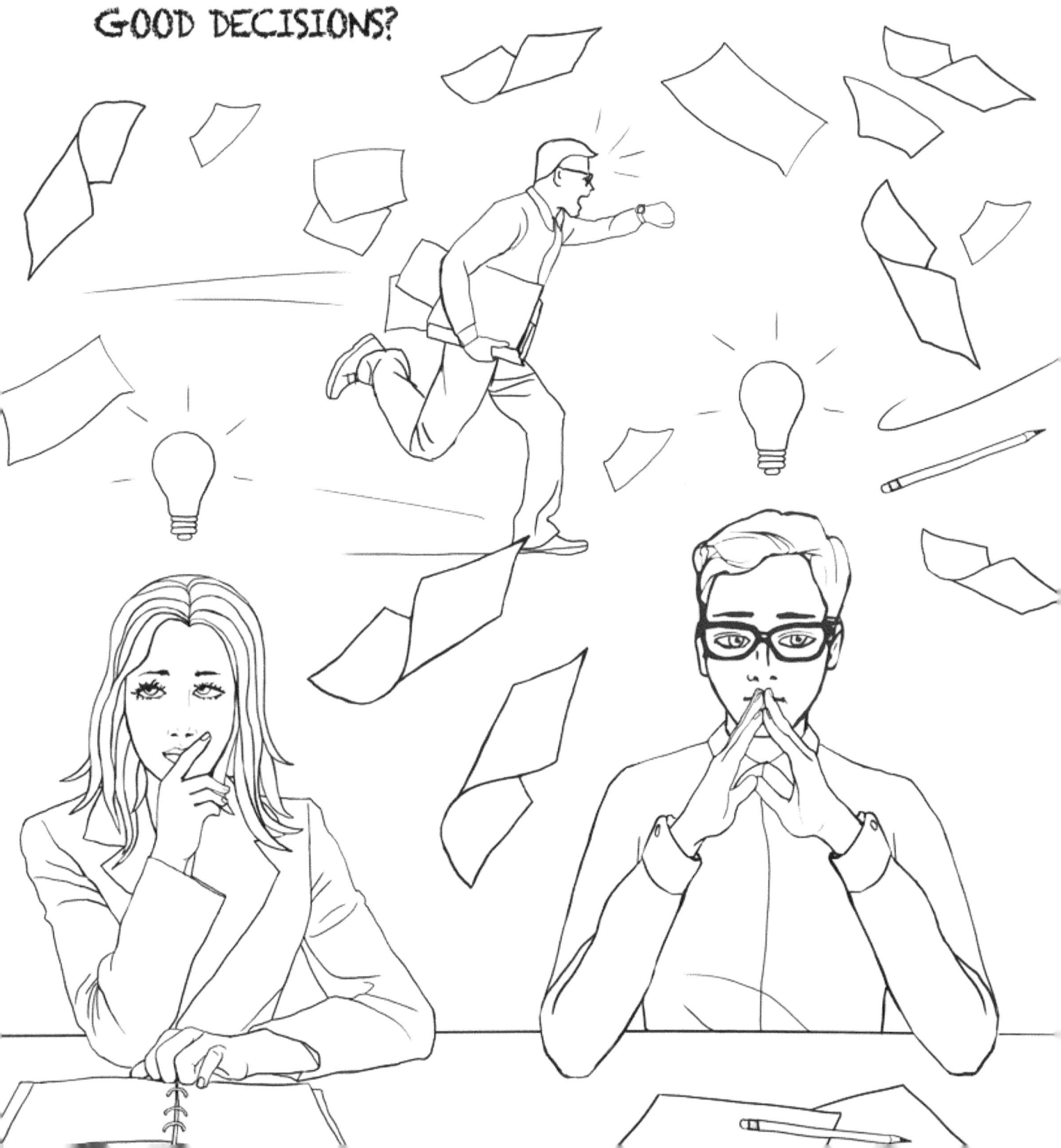

MAINTAINING A HEALTHY WORK – LIFE BALANCE IS A BIG CHALLENGE WHEN WE'RE ONLINE 24/7. TAKING WORK HOME ALL THE TIME CAN HAVE A NEGATIVE EFFECT ON YOUR PERSONAL RELATIONSHIPS. DO YOU FIND YOURSELF SACRIFICING SOCIAL LIFE OR FAMILY TIME TO FINISH WORK TOO OFTEN? UNPLUGGING AT THE END OF THE DAY CAN HAVE A POSITIVE IMPACT ON YOUR STRESS LEVELS.

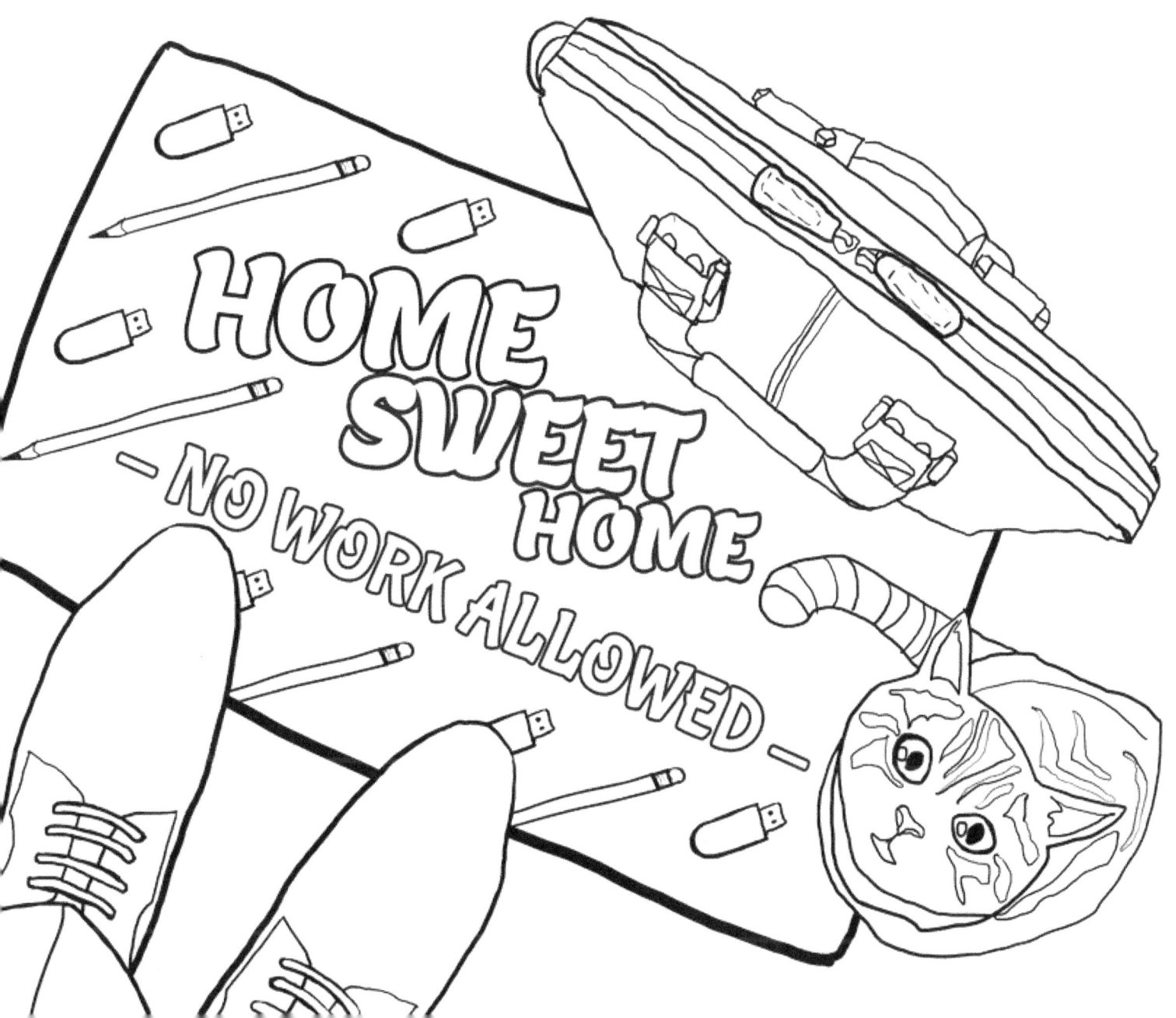

AHH, MEETINGS... DON'T WE ALL LOVE THEM?
UNPRODUCTIVE MEETINGS CAN TAKE UP A HUGE
PART OF YOUR WORK DAY AND LEAVE LITTLE
TIME FOR OTHER WORK.

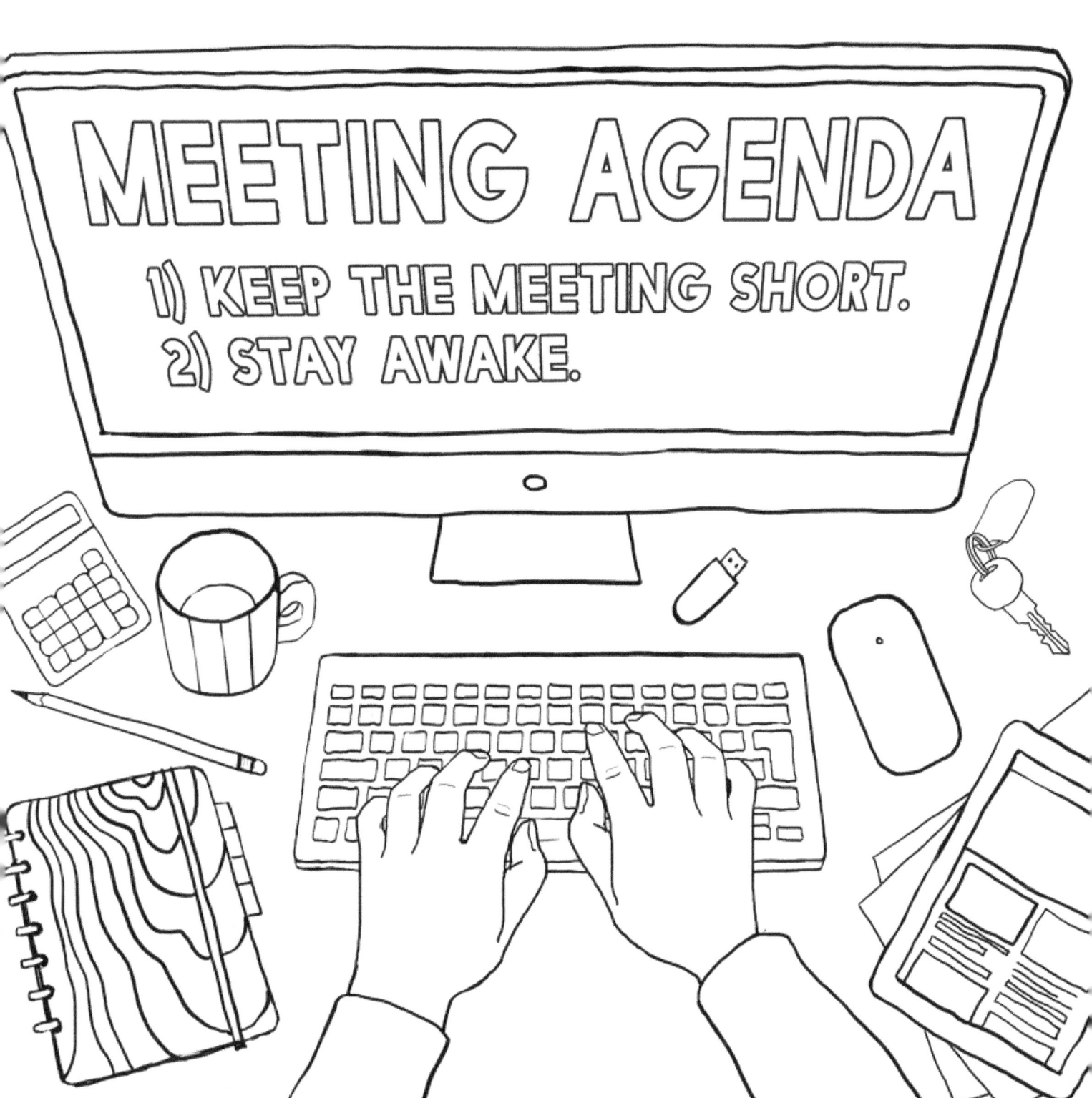

WHEN DEALING WITH A CRISIS IN THE OFFICE, IT'S IMPORTANT TO REMEMBER THAT YOU'RE NOT ALONE. YOU HAVE A TEAM THAT CAN SUPPORT YOU IF YOU REACT AND RESPOND APPROPRIATELY. WHETHER YOU TAKE ON A LEADERSHIP ROLE OR CHOOSE TO FOLLOW A LEADER, WORKING WITH YOUR TEAM TO RESOLVE STRESS AND COME TO THE RIGHT DECISION WILL BE CRUCIAL FOR COMING OUT OF A CRISIS SUCCESSFULLY.

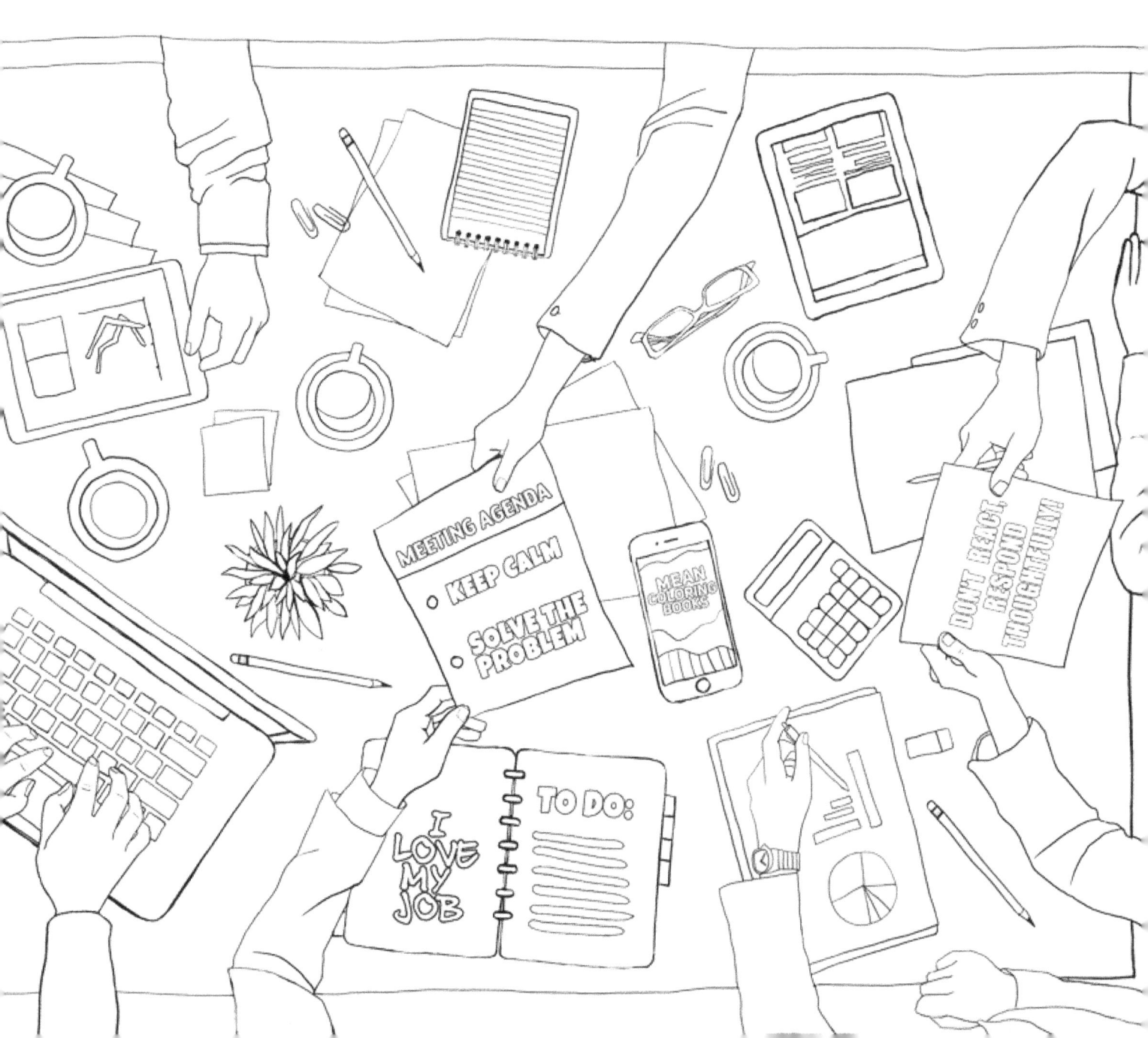

WHAT IS STRESSING YOU OUT TODAY?
WRITE, DOODLE, OR DROP A FEW TEARS.
GET IT OFF YOUR CHEST!

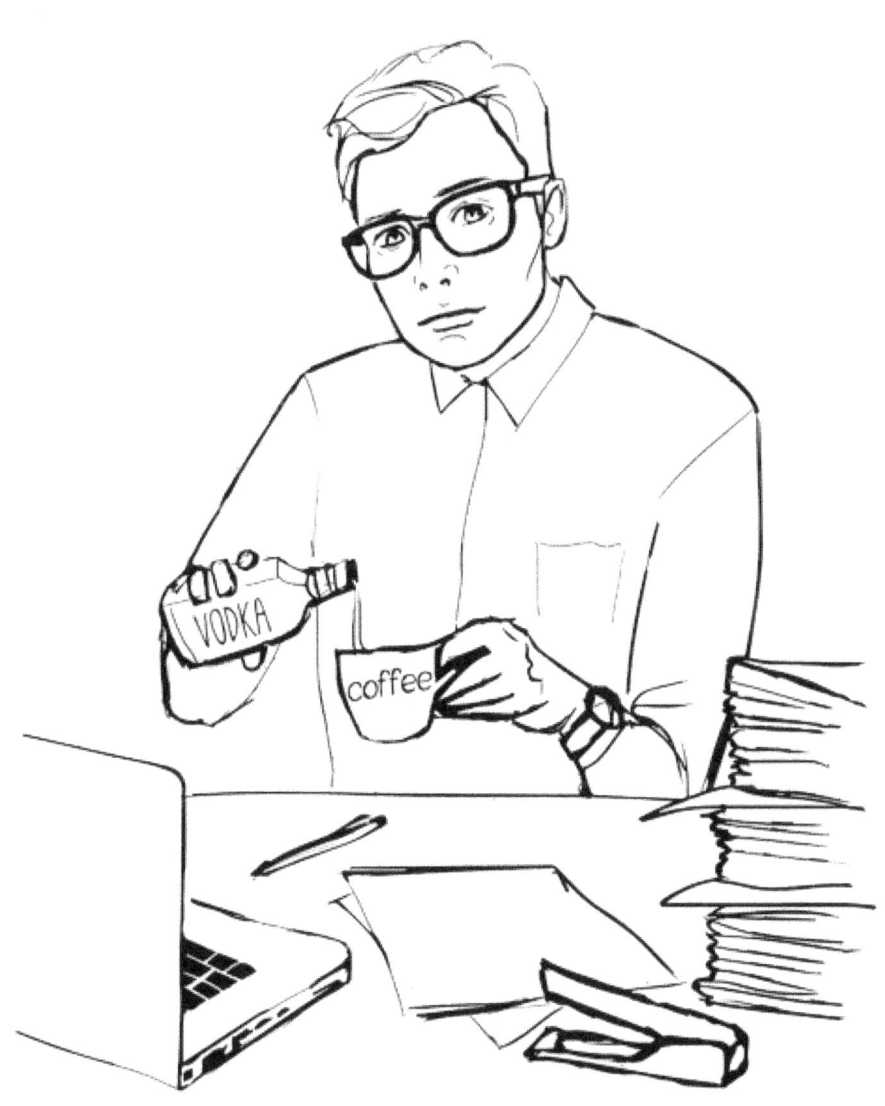